Sharing
the
Season

A Collection of
Christmas Warmth

by
Deborah Hansen

Cover Photo © Trevor Wood/Tony Stone Images
Cover Design and Typography by Roy Honegger

Published by Great Quotations Publishing Co.,
Glendale Heights, IL

Library of Congress Catalog Card
Number: 96-76125

ISBN 1-56245-274-6

Printed in Hong Kong

Table of Contents

Traditions

The Christmas Season

Every country has a slightly different idea of the Christmas Season. The Catholic Church's reckoning of the whole season stretches from Advent, four Sundays before Christmas, to Candlemas on February 2.

In Iran, they prepare for Christmas with a partial fast that lasts the entire month of December to Christmas Day.

Holland starts Christmas on the last Saturday of November, when St. Nicholas arrives by boat, and ends the festivities on the second day of Christmas, December 26th.

Spain begins festivities on December 8th with the Feast of the Immaculate Conception and doesn't let up until Epiphany.

Sweden stretches the holiday season for an entire month, from St. Lucia's Day on December 13th through January 13th.

The United States is one of the biggest exceptions to the rule. Our Christmas starts with Santa's Arrival at Thanksgiving and runs all the way through New Year's, or in some cases, January 6th.

Gift Giving

Gift-giving at Christmas goes back to Roman festivals of Saturnalia and Kalends. The very first gifts were simple items such as twigs from a sacred grove as good luck emblems. Soon that escalated to food, small items of jewelry, candles, and statues of gods. To the

early Church, gift-giving
at this time was a pagan
holdover and therefore
severely frowned upon.
However, people would not
part with it, and some
justification was found in the
gift giving of the Magi, and
from figures such as St.
Nicholas. By the middle

ages gift giving was accepted. Today, gift-giving is such an important part of our festivities that the whole year's budget has to be carefully planned to allow for the expense of Christmas presents. We have certainly come a long way from passing out evergreen twigs for good luck!!

Where did the Christmas Tree come from?

One popular legend of the origin of the Christmas tree involves an early Christian missionary St. Boniface. In the eighth century he was attempting to win the pagan Germans over the worship of Christ. One Christmas Eve in a great forest, he was shocked to come upon a

ceremony of human sacrifice
taking place at the foot of the
sacred oak tree of Odin at
Geismar. Seizing an ax, he
struck one great blow at the
tree, which was then toppled
by a great wind. The people
were awestruck and were
won over to Christianity,

12

but they felt lost without the symbol of their giant tree. St. Boniface pointed to a tiny fir tree that had nestled among the fallen oak and told them to take that as their sign that Christ was a bringer of life "ever green". The fir tree became his symbol.

Where do we get "X-mas"?

Xmas is an abbreviation
for Christmas. The X in
Xmas is actually the Greek
Letter Chi. Chi stood in the
language as a symbol for
Christ. The use of "Xmas"
as a simple abbreviation for
Christmas. It dates back to at
least the twelfth century and
has been in continuous
usage ever since.

When and where did lights come from?

In olden days candles were put on the tree to show the light of Christ. This was, of course, a fire hazard. Often buckets of water were kept around to douse the blazes that happened all too easily. The clever idea of electric Christmas lights first occurred to Ralph E. Morris, a New England Telephone Co. employee in 1895.

Strings of lights had actually already been made for use in telephone switchboards. Morris looked at the tiny bulbs and had the idea of using them on his tree. When the idea was introduced commercially, it caught on immediately and led to a great variety of shapes, sizes and colors and has vastly increased safety over the years.

Ornaments

The first Christmas trees
had fruit and flowers as their
ornaments. Cookies, nuts,
and other kinds of food were
later added. All of this was
so heavy it took a strong tree
to support all the weight.
German glass blowers found

a remedy to the problem by
blowing glass balls that were
very light to replace the
heavy fruit and cookies.
This was the beginning of
the highly specialized
industry that today produces
the myriad of Christmas
tree ornaments.

Red and Green—the colors of Christmas

Red and green are looked upon as the official Christmas colors, yet no one knows exactly why that is. The best guess is that they are the colors of holly. The bright red and green of leaf and berry seen in the cold whiteness of snow stand as a promise of the winter's end and spring to come.

Stockings

The custom of hanging up
a stocking to receive gifts
from Santa Clause probably
originates with a variant on
the St. Nicholas legend of
the three dowryless girls.
In this story, each time that
St. Nicholas threw the bag of
gold down the chimney, it
landed in a stocking that
happened to be hanging up
there to dry.

Trimmings and Such

Cinnamon Ornaments

1 1/2 c. Cinnamon
1 c. Applesauce

Mix ingredients and place
on a piece of waxed paper.
Spread the mixture out, and
cut with a cookie cutter.
Put a tiny hole at the top
with a small straw. Put a
ribbon through after the
ornament has set.

**Make that Mantel
Look Magnificent!**

Drape your mantel with a
striped runner you strew up
with flickering candles and
green boughs and flank with
urns and laden with dried
fruit over it all.

Christmas Card Decorations

Pin your cards to a 2″ wide ribbon vertical cut the ribbon about 36″. On the very top make a bow out of plaid ribbon. Looks lovely draped over doors all around the house!

Quick Dough Ornaments

2 c. baking soda
1 1/4 c. water
1 c. corn starch

Combine all 3 ingredients
and bring to a boil, stirring
constantly. Mixture will
magically turn into dough.
Put on a plate and into the
refrigerator to cool for a few
minutes. Then, knead dough
and roll 1/4" thick.

24

Cut out your favorite shapes with cookie cutters. (Don't forget to put a hole in the top, so ornaments can be hung later.) Let dry for 2 to 4 days. When dry, paint with stencil paint or any type of craft paint. Glue on sequins, glitter, etc., as desired. Put in string or ribbon to hang.

What to do with your stairway railing

Wind pine tree garland up the entire railing. Then wrap white lights in between the branches. Stand teddy bears all the way up the stairway with big holiday bows around their necks. Gives the house an inviting holiday look!

Liquid Potpourri:

Take a large saucepan and fill it half full of water. Add whole cloves, cinnamon sticks, orange rind and allspice, and gently simmer. The whole house fills with a wonderful aroma, and the mixture can be used again and again.

Bird food that's easy and fun to make:

Collect pine cones and spread with peanut butter. Roll them in birdseed and attach sting to hang outside.

Beautiful homemade ball ornaments:

Take glass ball ornaments and decorate with fabric scraps, sequins, ribbon etc. Great for the little ones!!

When sending holiday
cards sprinkle a little
potpourri into the envelope,
adds a wonderful touch!

To help get those smashed
bows back into shape try
curling with a curling iron.

Legend has it that by
burning a bayberry candle
on Christmas Eve, one
receives good luck
throughout the new year.

A Collection of Recipes

Sugared Nuts

4 c. walnuts
2 egg whites
1 c. sugar
1 1/2 t. cinnamon
1 stick butter

Spread nuts on cookie sheet and heat at 325° for 10 minutes. Beat egg whites until stiff peaks form. Fold in sugar and cinnamon.

After removing nuts from oven, fold into egg white mixture, put butter on the cookie sheet and allow to melt in oven.

Spread coated nuts onto the cookie sheet with the melted butter and stir, making sure they are coated well. Bake for 30 minutes, stirring every 10 minutes. Do not let them become too brown. Cool mixture completely and store in a sealed container.

Peanut Brittle

2 c. sugar
1T. butter
1/2 T. baking soda
1 can cocktail peanuts

Cook sugar over slow heat until caramelized. Remove from heat and add baking soda and butter. As it foams, stir in peanuts. Pour into a greased pan to cool. Break into small pieces.

Peanut Butter Bars

1 stick margarine
1 1/2 c. peanut butter
3 c. powdered sugar
4 T. butter
12 oz. chocolate chips

Blend margarine, peanut butter and powdered sugar. Pat into a 9"x 9" pan. Melt the chips and butter in a double-boiler. Spread into the peanut butter mixture. Refrigerate. Cut into squares.

Butter Cookies

1 lb. butter
2 c. sugar
8 c. flour
1 lb. margarine
1 egg

Mix ingredients together.
Use a cookie press or make
rolls and roll them in colored
sugar. Chill and slice. Bake
at 325° until just set or barely
golden brown.

*Chocolate-Covered Peanut
Butter Cracker Cookies*

Christmas sprinkles
Chocolate and white
  chocolate melting disks
Round, buttery crackers
Peanut butter

  Spread peanut putter
between two crackers. Dip
into melted chocolate and
place on waxed paper. While
still wet, decorate with
sprinkles and candies.

Poppyseed Bread

2 eggs
1 t. vanilla
1 1/2 c. sugar
1 t. baking powder
1/4 c. poppy seeds
1/2 c. oil
2 c. flour
1 t. salt
1 c. evaporated milk

Mix all ingredients
together with mixer. Pour
into 2 medium greased and

floured loaf pans. Bake at
350° for 1 hour. Test with
toothpick for doneness.
Makes 2 loaves.

Apple Bread

1 1/2 c. oil
3 c. flour
2 c. sugar
3 eggs
1 c. apple pie filling
1 t. salt
1 t. cinnamon
1 t. baking soda

1 t. vanilla

Mix all the ingredients together. Pour into a floured loaf pan and bake at 350° for 1 hour. Makes 1 loaf.

Shrimp & Crab Cheese Dip

1 lb. pasteurized process cheese spread
1 lb. unsalted butter
8 oz. crab
8 oz. popcorn shrimp

Heat cheese and butter in double boiler until melted. Add crab and shrimp. Dip with pieces of french bread, bagels or crackers.

Baby Baked Beans

1 lb. baby lima beans
3/4 lb. dark brown sugar
3 medium onions
1 lb. bacon

Soak beans overnight. Simmer beans with 1/2

onion until beans are tender.
DO NOT OVER COOK.
Drain. Layer: Beans, onions,
brown sugar and bacon.
Bake at 325° for 3 hours.
You may add a little dark
molasses for extra flavor,
according to taste.

Company Potatoes

5 lbs. potatoes
2 c. sour cream
8 oz. cream cheese
1/4 lb. margarine or butter

Wash, peel and cook potatoes until soft. Mix in an electric mixer and add sour cream, cream cheese and margarine. Mix until smooth, spoon into a greased 2-qt. casserole dish. Bake at 375° for 45 minutes, or until bubbly.

Songs and Poems

All I want for Christmas is My Two Front Teeth

This song was written in 1946 by Don Gardner. The song found true fame in 1948 when recorded by Spike Jones and his City Slickers for RCA Victor. This was one of the first major-selling Christmas novelty records. It presents no warm

Christmas sentiments, but does express an image that advertisers have found to be irresistible, a cute child with a gap in his front teeth.

Silver Bells

This song was introduced in 1951 in the movie, *The Lemon Drop Kid*, starring Bob Hope. The song incorporates the sounds and sights of Christmas in the city. The words were written by Jay

Livingston and music is by
Ray Evans. Bing Crosby
made it a hit.

Frosty the Snowman

This song was written in
1950 by Steve Nelson and
Jack Rollins. In 1951 it was
recorded by Gene Autry. In
1969 a TV Christmas cartoon
and record album were
made based on the story.

The Little Drummer Boy

This song was written in
1958 by Katherine Davis,
Henry Onorati and Harry
Simeone. This story is about
a little boy who travels to
Bethlehem to give the Christ
Child the only gift he
possesses, the ability to play
his drum. This song has
been the basis for two
animated television shows.

Jingle Bells

This carol, not mentioning Christmas at all, was composed in 1857 by J. Pierpont. Originally titled, *One Horse Open Sleigh*, it soon became known by the famous words of its refrain, "Jingle Bells".

Poems

A Christmas Carol
by Christina Rossetti

Before the paling of the stars,
Before the winter morn,
Before the earliest cock-crow
Jesus Christ was born:
Born in a stable,
Cradled in a manger,
In the world his hands
  had made
Born a stranger.

47

Priest and king lay fast
  asleep
In Jerusalem,
Young and old lay fast
  asleep
In crowded Bethlehem:
Saint and angel, ox and ass,
Kept a watch together,
Before the Christmas
  daybreak
In the winter weather.

Jesus on His mother's breast
In the stable cold,
Spotless Lamb of God was
    He,
Shepherd of the fold:
Let us kneel with Mary
    maid,
With Joseph bent and hoary,
With Saint and angel,
    ox and ass,
To hail the King of Glory.

The Bells
by Edgar Allen Poe

Hear the sleighs with the
  bells,
Silver Bells!
What a world of merriment
  their melody foretells!
How they tinkle, tinkle,
  tinkle,
In the icy air of night!
While the stars that over
  sprinkle

All the heavens seem to
   twinkle
With a crystalline delight;
Keeping time, time, time
In a sort of Runic rhyme,

To the tintinabulation that so
   musically wells
From the bells, bells, bells,
   bells, bells, bells-
From the jingling and the
   tinkling of the bells.

A Visit from St. Nicholas

The most famous as well
as most popular Christmas
poem of all was not even
meant to be published. On
the evening of December 23,
1822, the distinguished
scholar Clement Clarke
Moore recited for his
children a little something he
had composed. One of his
guests copied the poem and
the following year sent it

anonymously to the *Troy Sentinel* in New York, which published it on December 23, the anniversary of its composition. The description below it read:

"We know not to whom we are indebted for the description of that unwearied patron of children, but from whomever it may have come, we give thanks for it." The entire world soon felt the same, but Moore felt it beneath the dignity of an author of classical verse and a publisher of sermons. In 1844, Moore finally included the poem in his collected works, thus acknowledging his authorship.

'Twas the night before
Christmas, when all through
  the house
Not a creature was stirring,
  not even a mouse;
The stockings were hung
  by the chimney with care,

In hopes that St. Nicholas
 soon would be there;
The children were nestled
 all snug in their beds,
While visions of sugarplums
 danced in their heads;
And mamma in her kerchief
 and I in my cap
Had just settled our brains
 for a long winter's nap,
When out on the lawn
 there arose such a clatter,
I sprang from my bed
 to see what was the matter.

Away to the window I flew
    like a flash,
Tore open the shutters,
    and threw up the sash;
The moon, on the breast of
    the new-fallen snow,
Gave a luster of midday to
    objects below;
When what to my
wondering eyes should
    appear
But a miniature sleigh
    and eight tiny reindeer,
With a little old driver,

so lively and quick,
I knew in a moment,
    it must be St. Nick.
More rapid than eagles his
    coursers they came,
And he whistled and
shouted and called them
    by name:
"Now Dasher! now Dancer!
    now Prancer! now Vixen!
On, Comet! on, Cupid!
    on, Donder and Blitzen!
To the top of the porch!
    To the top of the wall!

Now, dash away, dash away,
dash away, all!"
As dry leaves that before the
wild hurricane fly,
When they meet with an
obstacle, mount to the sky,
So up to the housetop the
coursers they flew,
With the sleigh full of toys
and St. Nicholas, too.
And then, in a twinkling,
I heard on the roof
The prancing and pawing
of each little hoof.

As I drew in my head and
   was turning around,
Down the chimney St.
Nicholas came with
   a bound.
He was dressed all in fur,
   from his head to his foot,
And his clothes were all
tarnished with ashes
   and soot;
A Bundle of toys he had
   flung on his back,
And he looked like a
peddler just opening

his pack.
His eyes: how they twinkled!
  his dimples: how merry!
His cheeks were like roses,
  his nose like a cherry;
His droll little mouth was
  drawn up like a bow,
And the beard on his chin
  was as white as the snow.
The stump of a pipe he held
  tight in his teeth,
And the smoke, it encircled
  his head like a wreath:
He had a broad face,
  and a little round belly,

That shook, when he
laughed, like a bowl
   full of jelly;
He was chubby and plump,
   a right jolly old elf;
And I laughed, when I saw
   him, in spite of myself,
A wink of his eye and a
   twist of his head
Soon gave me to know I had
   nothing to dread.
He spoke not a word, but
   went straight to his work,

And filled all the stockings;
  then turned with a jerk,
And laying his finger aside
  of his nose,
And giving a nod,
  up the chimney he rose.
He sprang to his sleigh,
  to his team gave them
  a whistle,
And away they all flew
  like the down of a thistle;
But I heard him exclaim,
  ere he drove out of sight,
"Happy Christmas to all,
  and to all a good-night!"

Quotes for the Season

Another Christmas Miracle is how everyone receives more Christmas cards than he sends.

There are generally two kinds of Christmas gifts: the ones you don't like and the ones you don't get.

Why does the Christmas season come when the stores are at their busiest?

The Christmas season is only as meaningful as we make it.

When we throw out the Christmas tree we should be careful not to throw out the Christmas spirit with it.

Keeping Christmas is good, but sharing it with others is much better.

Christmas is a time to reflect upon the greatest gift of all.